VIA Folios 178

Fables From Italy and Beyond

Published by Bordighera Press, an imprint of the John D. Calandra Italian American Institute of Queens College, The City University of New York.

25 West 43rd Street, 17th Floor, New York, NY 10036

All rights reserved. Parts of this book may be reprinted only by written permission from the publisher, and may not be reproduced for publication in media of any kind, except in quotations for the purposes of literary reviews.

Library of Congress Control Number: 2025931701

Cover art by Grace Cavalieri.

© 2025, Grace Cavalieri & Geoffrey Himes

VIA Folios 178
ISBN 978-1-59954-228-7

Fables From Italy And Beyond

Grace Cavalieri and Geoffrey Himes

BORDIGHERA PRESS

*Grace and Geoffrey dedicate this book to each other,
once teacher and student, 50 years ago, now the best of friends.*

TABLE OF CONTENTS

Preface	9
The Third Voice	11

SECTION ONE

The King and the Woven-Willow Basket	15
The King, the Apple, the Prince, and the Widow	17
St. Joseph's Devotee	19
Olio d'Oliva	21
Fagiolo renale	23
No-Nonsense Nancy	25
Olio d'Oliva Does a Favor	28
The Peacock Feather	30
Quack! Quack! Quack!	32
Olio d'Oliva's Frightening Fortune	35
Sal Valentino	36
Sandrino	38
Three Balls and a Bowl	40
The Instant Astrologer	43

SECTION ONE

Two Brothers	49
Unpaid Debts	51
The Tree Frog	53
Orioles	55
The Widow's Dilemma	56
Dinner Party	57
Rescue/Capture	58

Canvas	59
The Magician	60
The Chase	61
Affliction	63
The Cliffs of Moher	64
The Long Way Home	65
Cat's Cradle	66
Mirror, Mirror, on the Wall	67
The Fairy and the Forester	69
Visitation	70
Black Dog	72
Mirrors	73
Palisades Manor	75
Past Present Future	77
Pretending	78
Prognostication	79
The Monk and the Rabbit	80
Safety	82
Saguaro	83
Icarus	84
Subjunctive	85
Take My Hand	86
This Solid Earth	87
A Year Later	88
The Story Without End	89
Acknowledgments	91
About the Authors	93

PREFACE

My great grandmother Graziella heard stories like the ones in this book from her great grandmother Guidita, who heard them from aunts and cousins before her. I'm sure Italo Calvino heard them from his elders too before he published his book, "Italian Folktales Selected and Retold." That's how Italian folktales survive. Other children may have sweet bedtime stories and lullabies, but ours were filled with arms and legs falling out of the chimney, parents abandoning their children in the forest, magical goose and peacock feathers, and lamb heads eaten for breakfast.

These tales have peppered my mind with fantasy and fable—and also the mind of my writer friend of 50 years, Geoffrey Himes. We decided we would write a truly collaborative book of poems—not merely mixing poems we'd written separately in the same volume, as some people do, but actually working together on each poem. Every poem in this book includes lines from each of us—and those lines have been revised so often that we no longer know who wrote what.

Geoffrey and I are very different writers—with different backgrounds, different personalities and different styles. We had to find some common ground, and we found it in fables, both oral and written, most particularly in the folktales of our mutual hero Calvino.

Human lives have a beginning, a middle and an end, so it makes sense that we would turn to similarly structured stories to explain our lives to others—and to ourselves. And when we add magic and surrealism to a tale, the exaggeration can clarify the reality we actually live in. Stories start privately, get altered as they're passed around and finally became legend.

Section One of this book includes the poems directly inspired by Calvino's folktales, while Section Two presents the poems indirectly inspired by Geoffrey and me , the stories that spring from the unplumbed wells of our mind. And when our two voices join into one, a third voice emerges that had never existed before.

Grace Cavalieri

THE THIRD VOICE

When a harmonica and a violin play
the same melody a fifth apart,
one soaks into the other.
A third voice emerges
that's neither mouth harp nor fiddle.

When two poets alternate
lines in the same poem,
each rides the cannonball of melody
but leans right or left to shift the trajectory.
One may go lower; the other higher.

A third note emerges creating a new chord,
never heard before yet strangely familiar.

—Grace Cavalieri & Geoffrey Himes
Maryland, June 2024

SECTION ONE

Italo Calvino's book *Italian Folktales*, a collection of short prose pieces based on ancient folk tales are here imaginatively adapted. Characters have been added and subtracted; plots have been changed, and the whole thing recast into poetry.

THE KING AND THE WOVEN-WILLOW BASKET

His advisors told him not to, but the king was young
and loved riding his piebald mare alone through the woods.
One day he came upon an ironwood fence,
so cunningly woven it was impenetrable.
Hmmm, the king said to himself,
such a fence must guard something valuable.
And just then the cherry-haired Fiorenza
popped up above the fence.
Are you a peddler? the young beauty asked.

Before he left, our father said we could
let down a basket to buy something from a peddler.
Why, yes, I am a peddler, the king lied.
I have a trinket here you might like to buy.
She lowered her woven-willow basket,
and the king climbed inside.
Oof, it's so heavy, Fiorenza said.

That's because it's so valuable, the king called.
Fiorenza asked her sisters, the raven-haired Clarenza
and the lemon-haired Innocenza, to help her pull the rope.
They huffed and puffed and the king came over the fence.

Finding not a trinket in the basket but an agile young man,
the sisters all but swooned. They smothered him with kisses,
and he invited the youngest, Innocenza, to come to the ball.
Off they went, her arms around the king on the mare.
The ball began with a banquet of lamb, venison and swan.
While the king and his friends ate lustily,
Innocenza sat with her chin in her palm,
thinking of her hungry sisters at home.

While pet monkeys swung from the candelabras
and servants in red uniforms refilled the plates,
Innocenza slipped away into the kitchen and stuffed a mutton leg
and a wine flask inside her blouse for Fiorenza and Clarenza.

Just then the pipes and violins struck up a tune,
and the king asked Innocenza to dance.
But when he embraced her, the white suet
and purple wine spilled onto his jacket.

The angry king called her a thief and a peasant
and ordered the steward to take her back home.
But at midnight, after the ball was over,
the king paced the cold, lonely castle floors.

Oh, you foolish king, his confidante Olio d'Oliva told him.
You don't know a good thing when you see it.
Caring about one's family is a good quality.
This is the girl you have been searching for.

His advisors told him not to, but the king was young
and loved riding his piebald mare alone through the woods.
And every day he returned to that ironwood fence,
so cunningly woven it was impenetrable.

THE KING, THE APPLE, THE PRINCE AND THE WIDOW

How I envy the apple tree, said the childless queen.
Each year it has so many children.
Olio d'Oliva heard her prayer and cast a spell.
The queen died in childbirth but gave birth to an apple.

It was a bright, red Honey Crisp apple
that never browned as the weeks went by.
The grieving king placed it on a throne of satin,
as green as an orchard's leaves.

The servants polished the apple twice a day
and carried it to bed on a silver platter.
But when the cathedral bells rang at midnight,
the fruit rose from bed as a flesh-and-blood woman.

For four hours she stood on her cold stone balcony,
her long red hair swinging across her ivory nightgown.
Let me remain a woman, she prayed to the silver moon,
But before every dawn, she turned to an apple again.

An insomniac prince rode past the castle at two in the morning,
spied the red-headed maiden and was instantly smitten.
The next morning, he called off his wedding to the Widow of Naples
and returned to the castle to meet the moonlight princess.

The jilted widow was furious and chased after her fickle fiancé.
When the prince and widow arrived, the king was puzzled.
I have no daughter, he said. My wife died in childbirth
and left nothing behind but a precious apple.

The prince and widow demanded to see the apple,
so the king led them up the spiral stairs.
Beneath the bed's brocade canopy,
the apple sat on its soft, plump pillow.

This apple, the prince sighed, gleams crimson like her hair.
You fool! barked the widow. Why do you praise
a piece of fruit as you never praised me?
She pulled a dagger from her sleeve and sliced the apple in two.

From the fruit spurted a geyser of human blood
and the cry of a woman in childbirth.
The red-headed princess stepped out of the apple
and into the arms of her long-suffering father.

The widow was banished to Naples.
The prince's proposal of marriage was accepted.
Olio d'Oliva, the king's advisor, gave her blessing,
and the king married the lovers beneath a blossoming apple tree.

ST. JOSEPH'S DEVOTEE

Alfonso was a carpenter who loved St. Joseph,
who was also a carpenter.
Alfonso gave all his alms
in the name of St Joseph.
Three times a day he prayed
to Saint Joseph
and named all his sons Joseph.

When Alfonso died and went to Heaven,
Saint Peter said, *No, you cannot not enter.*
You did nothing all your life but pray to St. Joseph
when you could have been doing great deeds
or at least praying to some other saints.
Alfonso begged and pleaded,
but St. Peter could not be swayed.

Finally Alfonso demanded
to see his patron saint.
When St. Joseph arrived, he shouted,
This is an outrage.
Let this man in at once.
He's my most faithful devotee.
But St. Peter could not be swayed.

OK. that's it, St Joseph said coldly.
I'm leaving and taking my wife and son with me.
What? St. Peter shouted.
What kind of heaven would this be
without Jesus, Mary and Joseph?
Exactly, said St. Joseph.
And finally St. Peter was swayed.

He blanched—and not in an angelic way.
Let's not get carried away, he purred.
There's been a misunderstanding.
Of course, Alfonso can enter heaven.
The heavenly carpenter took the earthly carpenter
by the arm and with triumphant grins,
marched into paradise.

OLIO D'OLIVA

She was short and round as a new rolled hay bale.
One eye blue, one brown. They seemed not to know
where they were rolling at any given moment.
These eyes did not scare the villagers,
but lured them closer, as if they were kibbitzing
as their children played with marbles.

They called her Olive Oil,
because she answered her neighbors' questions
by pouring the yellow liquid on the stone path
before her door and finding signs in the way it ran.
They paid her with baskets of mele and pera,
depending on the season.
She gave half of her food to her dog,
who also had one eye blue, one eye brown.

Barbaglia asked when she would
conceive a long-hoped-for child.
Olio d'Oliva poured the oil,
and Barbaglia swore she saw
an infant's shawl in the puddle.
Filled with tears, she kissed the fortune teller's bony hand.
Nine months later, she delivered a healthy girl,
She left warm baked bread daily
at the door of the magic hut
as long as her breasts dripped with milk.

Where Olio d' Oliva got such a supply
of oil was never questioned,
just as her predictions were never challenged,
just as her methods were never explained.
But how did she?
The local olive orchards had gone dry with a disease
that made leaves, twigs and fruit curl inward and blacken.
The women had gone barren from a bishop's curse,
and the river was so low children could walk across.
Yet the king had caskets full of olives;
the sorceress always had jars of oil
and her stone path was wet with answers.

FAGIOLO RENALE

Don Giovanni was starving.
His stomach echoed like a big bass drum.
He marched to that beat down a long dusty road
till he found a pale kidney bean in the dirt.

He was about to pop the bean in his mouth when he thought,
*No, I could plant this bean in a pot
and grow a plant that would give me lots of beans.*
So he stuck the bean in his pocket instead.

Soon he was dreaming of the farm he would have:
a barn stacked floor to ceiling with bushels of beans,
a three-story farmhouse with turrets and a porch
where he would welcome wealthy guests arriving in carriages.

If I'm going to be welcoming such guests, he told himself,
I'll need a better coat and a pretty wife to stand beside me.
In the shop window, he saw a handsome blue coat,
and he forgot about the bean in his pocket and the pot to put it in.

He admired himself in the mirror, and Annabella stopped to flirt.
Do you think I should buy this coat? he asked her.
It suits you well, she said, *but it must be expensive.*
I don't worry about money, lied the man with one bean in his pocket.

Wrap it up, he told the storekeeper, *and I'll return with the money.*
No, no, the owner said, *take it now. I trust you.*
So Don Giovanni took Annabella on the arm of his blue coat
and strolled through the town as if he owned it.

He dropped Annabella at her hotel with a kiss on the cheek.
Then he hurried to his employer, Olio d'Oliva, a rich farmer.
You can keep all the wages you owe me, said Don Giovanni,
if you do me one favor: Tomorrow, pretend that I own this farm.

Olio d'Oliva laughed like a horse and agreed to play along.
The next day Don Giovanni in his borrowed blue coat
showed Annabella and her mother the cattle in "his" fields,
the wheat in "his" barn, the fagiolo in "his" garden.

The eyes of the mother and daughter widened in surprise.
The mother asked the farm's income, and he made up a number.
Annabella took him behind the barn and kissed him.
A wedding date was quickly arranged.

With his dowry, Don Giovanni bought a pot for his bean,
then twelve more pots and then a barn.
Soon the barn was full of beans,
and the house was full of seven happy children.

Annabella forgave Don Giovanni all his lies,
although her mother never did.
And Annabella made Don Giovanni
wear his blue coat to church every Sunday.

NO-NONSENSE NANCY

They called her No-Nonsense Nancy,
because she didn't take shit from anyone,
not from her parents,
not from her siblings,
not from her children,
not from her bosses,
not from her customers.

One day she got an invitation for lunch
at the cobwebbed castle on the outskirts of town.
Don't go, her mother cried.
Everyone who visits there winds up dead.
I won't, said No-Nonsense Nancy.

She let herself in to the dark, dusty dining room,
sat down at the table and waited.
Whoosh! A left leg fell down the chimney into the fireplace.
A right leg followed, then two arms, a torso and a head.
She watched the body parts squirming in the ashes
as they connected to one another
and stood up as a tall Neanderthal giant.

Come with me, the giant roared,
but Nancy didn't take shit from giants either.
Not until you serve me the lunch you promised,
perhaps antipasti, lasagna and a glass of chianti wine.
The giant grumbled but he disappeared into the kitchen
and returned with a silver tray and good china.

He glowered as she ate slowly, savoring each bite.
Enough! the giant shouted.
Open that small door behind you and crawl through.
No, replied No-Nonsense Nancy. *You crawl through first.*
The giant grumbled more loudly yet,
but he got down on his hands and knees
and went through the door.
Nancy followed him and found him holding a burning torch
and standing at the top of a steep spiral staircase
of blackened iron where she might have tumbled to her doom.

He stood aside and said, *You go first.*
No, she said. *You go first.*
He did, but he had to cut the ankle-high tripwires as he went.
At the bottom of the double-helix stairs,
the giant pointed to a mildewed coffin and said, *Open the lid.*
No, Nancy said. *You open the lid.*
The giant opened the lid and quickly leaned backwards
as the booby-trapped arrows went flying.

Inside the coffin were three bags of gold—small, medium and large.
The giant said, *Carry them upstairs.*
No, said Nancy. *You carry them upstairs.*
The giant cut the red wires sticking out of each bag
and carried them up the spiral staircase.

You have passed the test, the giant sighed.
The small bag is for the ambulance
that is waiting outside to pick up your dead body.
The medium bag is for the village's poor.
The large bag is for you—and so is this castle.

No-Nonsense Nancy lived in the castle for a long time.
She never took shit from giants or dwarves,
and she never let anyone walk behind her.

She loved to go hunting in the castle woods,
and one day a bear attacked the camp.
All her servants told her to run for safety.
No, she said. *You go first.*
And that was the end of No-Nonsense Nancy.

OLIO D'OLIVA DOES A FAVOR

One night when the planets were parata—all in a line—
Olio d'Oliva heard a pounding on her door.
She wrapped herself in a cowhide hanging nearby
and opened the door to see old Marco,
a peasant she knew from down the road.

Marco sank to his knees, sobbing.
Having lost so many people to the influenza,
he needed to know exactly when he would die.

He had already written his will,
bequeathing his cow to his brother Alfonso,
his bedroom furniture to his sister Rosario,
and his orchard to his good neighbor Lucia.

So now there was much to do:
washing the cow's tail dripping with dung,
airing his mattress, showing Lucia how to prepare
the basilica and lemon trees for the coming frost.

Come back tomorrow, a yawning Olio d'Oliva told him.
*Tonight there is only a single handful of stars in the sky,
not enough light to see your fortune in the puddled oil.
Ritorna domani when the sun is shining,
and we can be more exact.*

She swept the hide around her as if to go.
No, no, Marco wailed, pulling on her hem,
*I haven't slept in fourteen nights, and I cannot last
even one more day without knowing—per cortesi comprendi.*
Olio d'Oliva sighed and poured the oil on the white stone path.

Marco stared down at the spreading puddle
and studied what he could see of his face.
A nose wriggled; an eye winked, lips pursed.

Just then a cloud blanketed the sky
and the picture disappeared.
Aha, said Olio d'Oliva. *See? Bene.
Your face is gone from the well of death.
The reaper is not interested in you for now.*

Marco exhaled in relief and wiped his eyes dry.
He was happy not to die and happier, perhaps,
not to have to part with his possessions.

He promised to bring Olio d'Oliva
a bowl of basil leaves and a pint of cow's milk
every Friday without fail.
She told him, *Maybe you should add Wednesdays.*

THE PEACOCK FEATHER

The shepherd created a cane fife
From the tallest reed in the forest.
He was stunned when the flute came to life
And out came this troubling chorus.

The king was lying sick in his bed.
Doctors needed just one peacock feather.
I had the cure; they left me dead.
Now I lie in the ground forever.

The song was the voice of the prince
Who six months ago disappeared.
There'd been no trace of him since.
What happened was now very clear.

A peacock flew out of a pine tree.
Down floated a long, green feather.
My brothers stole that prize from me.
Now I lie in the ground forever.

The people gathered and paid
To hear the song of the shepherd.
He enchanted each wife, every maid
With a tune that leapt like a leopard.

With knives my brothers all stabbed me
For the sake of a peacock feather.

And buried me with shovels three.
Now I lie in the ground forever.

The music rose up from the square
And in through the high castle window.
When the king heard that sweet air,
He called down to the piper below.

A reed grew up from my chest,
Where once there had been a feather,
A stalk that's taller than all the rest
Where I lie in the ground forever.

The shepherd, he gladly played
When he heard the gold coins a-jingling.
The king and queen were dismayed
To hear what their dead son was singing.

Father, father, I did my best
To bring you a peacock feather.
Mother, Mother, I am at rest
Now I lie in the ground forever.

The king and queen called their sons three
To hear the song of the forest.
The sons were carefree and laughing
Till they heard this awful chorus.

Oh, my wicked brothers three,
Why kill me for only a feather?
Why take the throne away from me
And leave me in the ground forever?

The king sentenced all three selfish sons
With an anger that sounded like thunder.
He cast them out of his green kingdom
And cursed them to always wander.

QUACK! QUACK! QUACK!

The king's banquet was in full swing.
Some were drinking, some were dancing.
Some were drinking, then dancing with comic results,
and everyone was laughing.

Everyone, that is, but the princess,
who sat stone-faced next to her father.
Why don't you laugh? the king asked.
I don't find anything funny, she replied.

It's true, the king said, *I can't remember
you ever laughing since you were born.*
And you never will, the princess said,
for this is not a funny world.

If I find a suitor who can make you laugh,
he said, *will you marry him?*
Yes, she answered, *but only if each suitor
is put to death if he tries and fails.*

All the banquet guests witnessed this bargain,
and news of it spread far and wide.
Many a princely suitor came with jokes and pratfalls.
And many a prince was put to death.

The news finally reached a tiny village,
where a poor cobbler had a son with terrible acne.
I'll go to the castle, the son said, *and make her laugh.*
No, no, no, said the father, *you'll die like the rest.*

But the son was stubborn and was halfway out the door
before the father said, *Wait a minute. It's a long way.*
Take these ducats, this loaf of bread and this pouch of wine.
Cock-a-doodle-doo, toodle-loo, the son said, but the father didn't laugh.

The son had only walked for three hours
when he met an old woman at a crossroads.
I'm so hungry, she said, and he gave her his bread.
I'm so thirsty, she said, and he gave her his wine.

I'm so poor, she said, and he gave her his florin.
You are so kind, she said. *Please take this goose in thanks.*
If the goose ever cries out, Quack! Quack! Quack!
you must quickly shout out, Stick to the back!

Now the boy was hungry, thirsty, poor and still had terrible acne,
but he did have a handsome goose with long brown feathers.
He stopped at an inn and begged for a room though he was penniless.
The innkeeper coveted the goose and gave the boy a bed in back.

At midnight, as the boy slept beside his goose,
the innkeeper's daughter crept in to steal the feathers.
Quack! Quack! Quack! cried the goose. *Stick to the back!*
cried the boy, and the girl's hand stuck to the goose.

Help! I'm trapped, cried the girl and her brother
came running and tried to pull his sister loose.
Quack! Quack! Quack! cried the goose. *Stick to the back!*
cried the boy, and the brother's hand stuck to his sister's back.

When the innkeeper saw the situation, he called for a priest.
The Holy Father mumbled a prayer and laid his hand on the wailing brother.
Quack! Quack! Quack! cried the goose. *Stick to the back!*
cried the boy, and the priest's hand stuck to the brother.

Just then a peddler of pots and pans who had a grudge
against the priest came by and whacked the clergyman on his spine.
Quack! Quack! Quack! cried the goose. *Stick to the back!*
cried the boy, and the peddler's hand stuck to priest.

The princess who never laughed was on her balcony,
when she saw the strangest sight: a peddler with pots and pans
stuck to a priest stuck to a boy stuck to a girl stuck to a goose.
It looked like a giant caterpillar with ten feet, eight arms and two wings.

The princess started to smile. She tried to pull down her mouth,
but she couldn't help herself. Soon her mouth cracked open
and out poured twenty years of stopped-up laughter at once.
She bent over and tears rolled out of her eyes.

This laughter like thunder filled the castle, and the king came running.
Who is the suitor who has made you laugh? her father asked.
The girl pointed to a shabbily dressed boy and dotted with pimples,
accompanied by a goose stuck to a girl, a boy, a priest and a peddler.

No way, the king roared angrily, but then he too began to laugh.
A deal's a deal, the princess said. She gave her new fiancé new clothes,
and she scrubbed his face with lye till his acne cleared up.
He was very handsome indeed and made a fitting groom for a wedding.

They lived in the castle a long time and became the king and queen.
And whenever the queen forgot how to laugh,
she went down to the stables, where they kept
a goose stuck to a girl, a boy, a priest and a peddler.

OLIO D'OLIVA'S FRIGHTENING FORTUNE

Olio d'Oliva was a scientist, it's true.
Her predictions were uncannily accurate.
But this fortune teller was also an artist.
When she poured olive oil on her stone path,
the pictures that came into focus were so detailed
you could count the loaves in the basket,
the strings on the singer's mandolin

and the blades of grass in the cemetery.
Today she poured the oil and saw a line
of people around the block near her house.
She followed them past the cobbler's shop and the baker's.
She followed them up the stone path and through the door.
She followed them to a casket resting on two sawhorses.
The lid was raised, and there was the future Olio d'Oliva,

her eyes closed and her hands folded across her bosom.
The present Olio d'Oliva immediately scraped her foot
across the picture in the oil,
scattering it into the nearby daffodils.
She cancelled all her readings for the week.
She locked the front door and hid in her bedroom.
What good is my talent, she asked herself,
if it only leads to this?

SAL VALENTINO

Sal Valentino was an excellent cobbler.
His shoes were as sturdy as they were handsome.
But his customers were as poor as he was
and often paid in cakes and pies.

One day a large, strong woman,
who walked ten miles every day carrying laundry,
paid him a sweet apple tart
for putting new soles on her old shoes.
Sal Valentino walked the woman to the corner and thanked her.

When he returned to his shop, the tart was covered in flies,
as if the crust were made of insects, not of flour.
The cobbler was furious, for his small payment was ruined.

He grabbed a leather strap from his workbench
and thrashed the tart again and again.
When the battle was over, he counted the casualties:
Five hundred dead and five hundred wounded.

He made himself a sloping leather cap,
and on the top he burned in the words,
Five hundred dead and five hundred wounded.
Everywhere he went, villagers wanted to hear the story.

Sal Valentino was tired of working hard for no money,
so he put on his cap and went to seek his fortune.
When he stopped at a tavern, a hideout for murderers and thieves,
They took one look at his cap and jumped out the windows.

The cobbler took a wrong turn on the path and entered
the Kingdom of the Amazons, forbidden to every male.
The warriors captured him, tied him with rough, skin-cutting rope,
and hung him upside down from an oak.

The Queen of the Amazons was the judge at his trial. She said,
Tell us how you killed five hundred and wounded five hundred.
Sal Valentino began to make up a story
about his exploits in the Battle of Calatafimi.

But once glance from the queen made him change his mind,
and he told the story of the apple tart and the houseflies.
Flies? You killed five hundred flies? Oh, my. And you admit it?
The queen roared with laughter and so did her warriors.

Because Sal Valentino, she continued, *is the first man
who ever told the truth to a woman,
he will become my first and only king
and will live with us in the forest forever.*

SANDRINO

Sandrino, the youngest of seven brothers,
slept on a mattress of dried corn stalks
with only a yellow curtain separating him
from his farmer father and laundress mother.

What can we do? his mama cried.
No food in the cupboard, no coins in the purse.
We can't feed them all, his papa said.
I'll take the oldest into the woods and leave them.

The woods nearby were full of bear and bobcat,
and Sandrino feared for his older siblings.
So he followed his father and his brothers
and dropped a white stone every ten steps.

Wait here, the father told his sons,
while I go hunting for funghi.
He ran off, and Sandrino came out of hiding.
Come with me, he said, and they followed the stones home.

The parents were shocked and unhappy
when the brothers came through the door.
But they quickly put on big smiles and cried,
We're so happy that you're safe.

The next morning, the father told the oldest sons,
I know a better place for funghi. Follow me.
Again Sandrino trailed behind, but he had no more stones.
So every ten steps, he dropped a bread crumb.

Wait here, the father told his sons,
while I go hunting for funghi.
He ran off, and Sandrino came out of hiding.
Come with me, he said, but crows had eaten the crumbs.

Sandrino pretended he knew where he was going,
but he was walking in the wrong direction.
Soon he and his three older brothers were hungry and thirsty,
stumbling through underbrush that tore their white shirts.

Finally they came to a creek where they drank their fill.
Across the creek was a field of funghi where they ate their fill.
These are best funghi I've ever tasted, Sandrino said.
We could sell these in the city for many gold coins.

They stuffed their pockets with fleshy, blond funghi
and found a sign that read, "Padua four miles."
The fat cook with a high hat at the fancy restaurant
tried a funghi and quickly bought the rest for 100 gold coins.

The brothers wanted to go home, but Sandrino said, *No, wait.*
Our father twice took us into the wood and left us there.
Let us pool our money to buy a house here in the city
and to start our own mushroom business.

And that's what they did. Each married a pretty plump wife,
and each wife had four plump, happy sons,
and the fathers never took those sons
into the woods to abandon them.

THREE BALLS AND A BOWL

He was a good king but vain.
Every morning he faced the mirror and sang:

Mirror, mirror, shining bright,
Tell the truth in reflected light.
I am handsome, as you can see.
Are any out there as fair as me?"

One day, the mirror, tired of this,
answered him with a song of her own:

You are handsome, yes, it's true,
but one is better looking than you.
The King of France has a teenage son
who glows as bright as the morning sun.

Soon the vain king and all his calvary
were crossing the Alps into France.

Meanwhile, his wife was pacing the floor.
She was a good queen but proud.
She thought that she had married
the handsomest man in the world.

When the king reached the palace in Paris,
the young prince greeted him and it was true:

The teenage boy had the skin of a ripe peach,
hair with golden curls like wood shavings.
Meanwhile, the proud queen lay in Italy,
dreaming of a prince with sun-drenched skin and hair.

In France, the vain king was furious but hid it well.
He smiled and talked pleasantly about
jousting and illuminated manuscripts.
It was an amiable afternoon and the prince said,

Here are three magic balls, drop them into a bowl
of pure milk and I'll visit you wherever you are.

When the vain king returned home, he told his wife:
Bring me a bowl of milk untainted since it left the udder.
She did, and the king dropped in the balls—plop, plop, plop.
The prince of the Paris palace and of the queen's dreams appeared.

The three monarchs talked and laughed over wine and cheese,
but the vain king noticed the flirting looks between queen and prince.
The following week, king prepared the bowl of pure milk,
but this time he added broken glass,

so when the balls were dropped and the prince arose,
he was covered in dozens of bleeding cuts.
The prince cried out like a wounded cat.
The proud queen roared like an enraged lion.

She was so angry, in fact, that she grabbed
a sword and chopped off the vain king's head.
Slowly she peeled off the prince's bloody clothes
and carefully picked the glass from each wound.

The prince was amazed at her sure, gentle touch.
As the cuts began to close, his heart began to open.

The king's advisor, Olio d'Oliva, told the queen:
Pour honey into each cut and seal it with lemongrass.
Wait ten days and his skin will be smooth as a baby's bottom.
Then you can marry him as you so obviously desire.

A month later, at the wedding reception, the queen told Olio d'Oliva:
Once again I am married to the handsomest man in the world.

THE INSTANT ASTROLOGER

The King of Mantua had lost his ruby ring,
left to him by his father and his father's father.
He looked everywhere but could not find it.
He had heard of the seer Olio d'Oliva

and assumed she was an astrologer.
Perhaps she could read the stars and locate the ring.
He had such great faith in the heavens
that he even owned a telescope.

Olio d'Oliva had many talents
but reading the stars was not among them.
Yes, the planets she could see,
but the stars were too far away.

Yet the king's promise of great gold tempted her.
How hard can it be to become an astrologer?
she asked herself. *Just look up in the sky
instead of down on the ground.*

So she was brought to Mantua
and ushered to the throne.
Here I am, Your Majesty, she said,
Olio d'Oliva, the astrologer.

She peered through the telescope
and muttered, *Hmmm, I see.*
She was trying to make some sense
of those mystifying millions of stars.

Meanwhile three servants
behind a hedge were worried
about the new astrologer.
What should we do? one said.

*The stars are sure to tell her
we climbed through
the king's window to steal the ring.
The stars are high and see everything.*

Maybe we should confide in her, said another.
*If we throw ourselves on her mercy,
she may help us keep
our heads on our shoulders.*

So they sought out Olio d'Oliva,
the supposed astrologer.
Don't turn us in, they cried,
"*we're common folk like you.*"

Olio d'Oliva wanted the gold, so she said,
*I won't turn you in if you do exactly as I say.
Take the ring to the farmyard
and make the fat red chicken swallow it.*

Olio d'Oliva went to the King and said,
*I have studied the stars quite carefully
and I know just where the ring is.*
She ordered the fat red hen brought in

and its stomach slit open.
And there it was: a jewel as red as blood.
The king was so delighted that he ordered
two bushels of gold wheeled in to pay her.

They celebrated with a banquet of crayfish.
Delicious, she said. *"What is the secret of the sauce?"*
You're an astrologer, the king he answered,
You should be able to divine it.

Olio d'Oliva looked at the food, then the gold,
then back at the food. *Oh, Olio d'Oliva,
what have you gotten yourself into?* she mumbled.
Olio d'Oliva. Olio d"Oliva. What shall I do?

That's right! the king shouted.
*The crayfish are swimming in olive oil.
No one but an astrologer
could know such a thing.*

Our fortune teller returned to her village,
her donkey cart filled with gold coins,
and no one in the village
ever went hungry again.

And every night Olio d'Oliva stared
at the sky trying to find meaning
in all those millions of
bright sparks of light.

SECTION TWO

Modern folktales.

TWO BROTHERS

Two brothers, one handsome, the other ugly,
lived in a cottage behind the brambles.
One day a wandering fisherman
heard a tenor voice singing through the shutters,
a song to thrill the trees and make the flowers bloom.

The fisherman knocked upon the door,
greeted by an old woman with twigs in her hair,
cats swimming in and out of her skirt.
The fisherman had a daughter
who needed marrying before she was too ripe.

The Runey woman smiled and said,
I have two sons—come in here, boys.
They stood side-by-side by the timbered wall.
One, tall with golden ringlets like the sun,
the other twisted and pockmarked like the moon.

The mother said, *You can have either boy*
for a purse that spills a hundred golden coins
each time it opens, a tomato plant that bears
fruit all year long, and a pair of magic boots
that run faster than the wind.

Alas, the fisher said, *This is not a fairy tale,
and I cannot give what I do not have.
What I do have is a leather satchel
containing fifty golden coins
and a basket of fresh caught fish.*

For that price, you can have the tall one,
the woman said, with a downcast look.
The fisherman thought, *The old lady's mad as a cock,
giving away one whose ringlets glimmer in light,
whose eyes are as blue as the waters I fish.*

The fisherman dragged the boy at a furious pace
out of the woods, through the lavender fields,
over the rocky ridge and down to the sea.
Only then did he ask the panting boy,
Would you like to meet your bride?

The fellow's sculpted mouth opened
and what came out was a toad's croak.
His high head, his lithe limbs, his muscular legs
had the grace of a deer, but his voice was
covered in warts and full of dead flies.

That old witch cheated me, cried the fisherman.
I'm going to get my coins and fish back.
He grabbed the boy's wrist again and back they went,
over ridge, through meadows and into the woods.
But where the cottage had been, there was only a pond.

From deeper in the darkening woods, however,
from the shadows where no trail led,
came that familiar velvet voice,
like beer to the squirrels, whiskey to the rabbits
and wine to the frolicking, mocking birds.

UNPAID DEBTS

The low morning
sun paints tree-trunk
stripes
across the leaf-matted
slope.
The lonely witch,
the color of fallen leaves,
moves through the woods
invisibly
to surprise her debtors.
Such as me.

It started with the purchase
of one memory to fill a hole in my
past.
But it faded too fast,
as such thoughts do,
so I bought another and
another,
until she was drained of history
and I of
gold.

I still owed her for the childhood
birthday party.
Her anger stirred the leaves into a
funnel
and opened a vertical gash in an ancient
oak.
She shoved me inside and sealed the
wound.

Now I am casting the shadow
across the forest floor,
my roots thirsting for the
past,
my branches clawing at the
future,
my voice crying out to the witch,
Don't leave me
on the brink of
remembering.

THE TREE FROG

The tree was wounded
where lightning
had struck a branch.
Worms and woodpeckers
created a hole
just large enough
for an orange tree frog
to emerge
glowing like a lantern.

I held it in my hand,
its long purple toes
tracing the broken lines
in my palm.

What am I to the forest
and the forest to me?
Roots and branches
reach into me and out from me
through words and birds.

Slimy as spilled juice, his freckled back
is sweating poisons. His bulging eyeball
tracks the sleeve of my orange parka
to the collar and my foreign face.

Down the twin spiraling staircases of DNA,
one step is shared by me and this frog.
It might be a link of fear.
It might be a bond of affection.

The frog leaps from my hand
into the hole in the tree,
stares back with bottomless black eyes,
beckons me to follow.

ORIOLES

Who left the lamp burning?
Who knocked it over?
Who caged a tiny oriole?
When did it stop singing?

At the fulcrum of the hinge-shaped roof,
the oriole's mate is silhouetted by morning,
orange feathers the color of flame
ruffling under the sun's suspicious eye.

The rooms beneath this mansard roof,
loosened by fire, rinsed by hoses,
fill our noses with wet ashes,
pepper our yard with blackened furniture.

This bird was seen, so people said,
darting in and out of the attic ventilator,
flaming in orange, blushing in orange.
And in the rubble, a bent, empty cage.

How can we answer these questions
when each day we reinvent this world?
The sun glows orange behind the horizon.
The bird flies free.

THE WIDOW'S DILEMMA

Someone loves me more than I love him.
He brings me chocolate-covered caramels,
and oh how tempting are those caramels.
He knocks on my door on a Sunday.
Before I can make an excuse, he's inside.
As I'm boiling the water for tea,
he argues that poetry is really prose,
and prose is really poetry.
He tells me that trees are imaginary,
that I am beautiful, and he is young.
At the door, he leans in for a kiss,
but I turn my cheek just in time.
He pulls from a pocket his mother's ring.
He loves me more than I love him.
but after all, I do love sweets,
compliments and sparkling things.

DINNER PARTY

There is one chair empty at the table.
We all pretend not to notice.

But in our heads, we count the guests at cocktails
and rack our brains for who we've lost.

Over soup we discuss the cold weather,
but why can't we remember the names?

Was there a short woman in a red gown?
Was there a stout man in a white beard?

Over the entrée, we argue about the election,
but which of us is missing?

There's a shadow in the chandelier
with black wings and a silver blade.

During dessert, the candles are lit.
The flames flicker though the windows are closed.

RESCUE/CAPTURE

A white-throated sparrow at my feet,
beating one healthy wing against the dust
as if asking for my help.

I scooped her up in cupped fingers
and marveled at such beauty:
her snowy bib, her golden eyebrows.

Beware of holding
so much goodness
in your hand.

The darkening expanse
spread across the hills.
The tangled trees called for her.

A scattering of snow around us.
Her one wing flapped in my grasp.
Her earnest heart palpitated against my palm.

Beware of holding
so much goodness
in your hand.

CANVAS

The first color on the canvas was blue.
the color of grass at night
You asked me why.
I changed it to red, and you turned away—too bright you said.
I painted the sky green and the grass orange.
You peeled the orange and threw away the skin.
You stepped into the painting
and shrank to a silhouette on the horizon.
Goodbye, goodbye, you said.
I knew if you looked back at me, you'd return.
Night fell, and you were lost in misty mauve.
so I painted a creamy three-quarter moon,
and your face shone like a dime over your shoulder.
My brush rose like the sun, casting shadows across the paint.
You grew larger and larger filling the canvas.

THE MAGICIAN

The daffodil new in bloom is easy to love,
but save some love for when it turns to brown.
The architecture, though frailer, is the same,
The blossom is faded but the stem is strong.

I knew a man in a ragged, tweed coat.
His beard was snowfall; his back an archer's bow.
We made fun of his stumbling gait,
his door-creak voice and marbled eyes.

We hurled pebbles and insults till he turned toward us,
reaching into his pocket as if for a weapon.
He pulled out a velvet pouch, untied it,
and a mouse emerged in a tiny fedora.

From his other pocket came a canary in a bonnet.
The mouse and canary waltzed up one arm and down the other.
We crowded around and said, *More! More!*
But he scooped them into his pockets and walked away.

He whistled a tune that grandmothers love,
and we followed him into the woods,
where the yellow daffodils were closing down
while the red tulips were opening up.

Night after night, all we could hear
were our mothers calling us home
for supper till their voices were
faint as a whistle.

THE CHASE

Flying down the slippery stairs,
galloping across the drawbridge,
fleeing the castle ramparts,

first the peasant, then the princess,
he in a pair of patched-up boots,
she on a gleaming mare.

On they go, on they go,
across windblown waves of wheat,
past winding vines of grape.

Beneath his ragged burlap jacket,
in his drawstring leather pouch
is the elixir they both crave.

Yesterday that tapered vial
sat on her boudoir dresser
till grabbed by a stealthy hand.

Distance and time collapse to motion
down one creek bank, up the other,
sunflowers turn as they go by.

The peasant crouches in the briars.
The mare goes stampeding past.
The sun falls helplessly to night.

Neither one has thoughts of sleep.
He needs that medicine for his wife.
She needs it for her mirrored reflection.

Desperation is the daughter of despair.
It's a breathless run through coarse sharp grass.
It's the cold wind lifting a rider's hair.

We know who will win at the story's end
after all the brambles and the stones—
the one who has a horse and can call for more.

AFFLICTION

It was mostly my fault. I can see that now. I wanted
to believe that silk and silver could blend, something shimmering
that might complete us,
scissors that could cut scarves, scarves that could bind blades.
My hands were hard as steel, yours soft as satin,
both sleek and shining in the cold.

Last night was nine weeks long.
I'd fallen into the well on my own.
I climbed the ladder on my own.
I couldn't wake from the gloom,
practicing blindness, dressing in the dark,
holding my breath to see if even the dead would notice.
The sun's rays were sleeved and gloved.

I confess it is all my fault.
Now, I found what was lost: the missing sequence of bird calls, your touch
breaking the spell in the first thin line of light.
The sky in the east is reddening now, the blankets thrown off,
the numbers returned to the clock
as we wake to each other, for the last time, again, as we try one more time
and let the dead go back to their sleep.

THE CLIFFS OF MOHER

Across the turquoise meadow, bluebells tangled in her skirt,
she climbed the corner stile through burrs and twining vines.
Bundles dropped behind her, steam from a passing train.

Like the blue and fettered skies, clouds gathered in her eyes.
She was wild as the moors and cliffs on West Ireland's shore,
singing her song high and elusive like a lark caught in the brush.

Her elders were left spread on their tattered couch,
and she ran with red-stained hands and she didn't look back.
I crouched, still as moss behind the lichen-spotted wall.
I swear I saw it all.

THE LONG WAY HOME

I wanted to return with more than I had.
Three highways to go home:
the scenic, the straight and the strange.

My pants rolled up, cuffs heavy with gravel.
A beggar's bowl filled with snow
A cow gave birth, not caring who saw.

I kissed a girl behind a barbed wire fence
in the valley of happenstance
beyond the vale where no man goes.

Was this the road to heaven?
Behind the hedgerows on Chalk Hill Road
a beggar and a king shared a brew.

A goat herder wrapped me in his coat
five days after and several moons past
a chill caught me by the throat.

Ten two-lane blacktops, and fifty dirt tracks,
fiddles and stews unmentioned in guidebooks,
down the skinny, crooked roads,

One thousand and one white birds,
songs of protest and promise
strapped to my backpack.

CAT'S CRADLE

At night the tomcats prowl.
One followed her home,
climbed atop her armchair as if a jungle branch.
She strokes his belly,
feeling for the bottom of sorrow.
She sees the claws ready to spring,
hears the upholstery tearing.
He unbuttons her blouse.

Always the same surprise.
The wish is stronger than the past.
The setting sun wears a crimson hat.
The moon wears a swollen face.
Cats are mewing in her bed.
Cats are crying in her head.
So soft the fur, so soft the purr.
Red scratches on unsuspecting skin.
When the moon was full,
he was gone.

MIRROR, MIRROR, ON THE WALL

I never knew the difference between "then" and "now"
until I found the Mirror of Ten Thousand Days.

I suffered a dozen small cuts from briars and broken windows,
but I made my way inside the abandoned mansion.

There it was, beneath the bronze sconces,
hanging on the brocade wallpaper, the oval mirror.

I ran my fingers across the surface and they slipped through,
as if the mirror were the clearest river.

As they plunged in, my hands changed, grew younger,
ten thousand days younger, twenty-seven years younger.

My wedding ring was gone; the wrinkles were gone.
The red fingernail polish of my youth returned.

I followed my hands into the mirror, into a past
I was remembering accurately for the first time.

I climbed the stairs of my parents' house
to an attic and a hallway of doors I'd never seen.

One opened on a cramped bathroom with black-and-white tiles
and over the sink a wooden medicine cab with a beveled mirror.

I crawled into that mirror and was fifty-four years, twenty thousand days in the future, an old woman with shaky hands in an echoing apartment.

In that apartment was a corner vanity with a folding screen of three mirrors. I dove through the left-hand one and found myself in a castle.

Where was I? What year was it? My hands could have been any age. Then was now. Now was later. Later had already happened.

I walked into an empty ballroom, covered floor-to-ceiling, frame-to-frame with mirrors with no clues to where they led.

I picked one with a glowing, golden frame and I somersaulted into the mansion where I started. I could smell the mildew and mouse droppings.

I turned from the mirror and found the front door. The briars remained. A cool vanilla dawn beckoned from the horizon.

THE FAIRY AND THE FORESTER

She arrived, tiny silver feet first, wings blurring,
Why do you cut down my trees?

He leaned on an axe, chewed a twig
Here you are, starring in a poem on a page,
and to have paper, I have to cut down trees.

Her green eyes flashed like Aleppo Pines,
cheeks flushing with pink pique.
But the whole forest? just for paper?
She leaned in closer with her honeysuckle breath.

His forehead touched hers, and with his rum filled voice:
I love these trees. I hike in them. I hunt in them.
I sleep under their shade, shelter beneath their hovering hands.
But like so many others in this world turned factory,
to feed my children, I have to murder what I love.

The wood sprite pointed out beige-brown mushrooms
crowding the tree's base, translucent cobwebs
strung between leaves. She flew across pages to branches
brushing kisses that hung dew drops from spider cables.

The lumberjack, lifted his creaking, jean-cased knees
and stepped into the book, followed his winged friend
farther and farther into the forest as rain began its patter.

His guide looked over her shoulder to see he was still there
and dived deeper into the poem than anyone had ever gone.

VISITATION

A woman with flowers in her hair, flashes through the streets.
She stops at the road, gate, porch,
strides through front door, living room, dining room
to the old-sweater-comfort of the kitchen,
where the soup simmers in her eyes.

How many times has she come to this empty house
with its worn-out smells,
tobacco, dust and sausage? How many
days has she entered without permission,
the rusting key still working?

Outside, the moon shivers behind winter trees,
silhouettes bend beneath umbrellas.
In the remembered tureen,
peas split in a chain reaction;
bringing diced ham and memories bubbling to the surface.

Memory of a daughter's cry upstairs,
memory of a quickly abandoned bed,
memory of two men, young and old,
fighting in the kitchen, blade and hot grease.
Fifteen years upended in fifteen seconds.

What is the price of a moment's desire? the moonlight asks.
Taking the knife, she runs through the garden,
looking back just one last time,
seeing husband, teenage lover in dispute,
a child calling from the murky window.

BLACK DOG

We abandoned her in the long ago rain.
Everything we didn't love
is still in the house.

Here comes a dark and dangerous dog
scratching at the door.
Don't let him in.

A woman lives in the attic,
though we didn't invite her,
and we don't want her.

The dog barks out her name.
We push aside the curtain.
Yellow eyes stare through the glass.

When visitors hear footsteps,
we make up stories
about raccoons and squirrels.

Does the dog belong to the woman?
Does the dog belong to us?
Will this rain ever stop?

A memory in every dream.
A woman in every attic.
A dog at every door.

MIRRORS

In the maroon room she knows so well,
she's a top spinning with eyes shut tight
round and round and round and round
between the mirrors and the twelve-foot wall.

Every mirror shows a different self.
There she is, then someone else.
Maybe if she turns fast enough,
all those selves will become one.

But no, the more she twirls,
the more her selves multiply,
each with different clothes and hair,
each with a different secret wish.

Her friends and neighbors
press noses against the window panes
to watch the dancing women,
all different but all the same.

But who can say each image
is not another self? She believes.
She's here and then she knows
she's over there – that makes two of her—

and then to the left, that makes three,
and twirling again makes six.
No one can stop her, and who would even try?
Someone once told her she was not enough.

PALISADES MANOR

Where's the door we came through?
It was there last night by the coatrack.
Now nothing but plaster and copper sconces.
We run our fingers above the wainscotting
from corner to corner, not a crack.
We must have fallen asleep on the sofa
after a bottle of wine and a pipe of hemp.
We hardly know each other, and here we are.
The window is locked and the glass won't break.
The phones don't work, and we're out of food.
Water issues from the baseboard,
first a seeping, then a trickle.
We circle the perimeter, but there are no clues.
We shout at the ceiling, but no one answers.
We hurl our shoulders at the walls.

We fall back exhausted, sober at last, on the couch.
We only have ourselves, but what do we have?
The usual inquiries, then the unusual ones:
Tell me when you were scared like this as a child.
Tell me where you'd like to be if you weren't here.
If you could have any food right now, what would it be?

Let's be rational and make a plan.
Stand up on my shoulders, he says,
and reaches for the high vent.
Don't wobble underneath me, she says.
Careful, he says, *your heel's on my neck.*
The vent is locked and screwed shut besides.
She slides down his front, starts to topple, grabs hold.
They clinch a minute too long, turn away quickly.
One, two, three, he says, and they lift the couch.
No escape there, and they set it back.
They both bend over in pain and laugh at each other.
There's nothing more we can do now.
Let's sleep this off and try again in the morning.

When they awake, the door is there again.
They cautiously open it, poke their heads into an empty hallway.
They look at each other, head off in different directions.

Three steps later, they turn around and stare.

PAST PRESENT FUTURE

The man on the train looks back.
Parallel lines, they say, never meet,
but these do—a dot on the horizon.

There they stand, that familiar scene:
men in hats, hands in pockets,
as if waiting for the past to return,

blackbirds on every shoulder,
small patches of black
swirling and swooping.

On the depot wall, the schedule tells us
where we've been, where we're going.
But the crows have other plans.

The man on the train looks forward now.
A woman flings out her arms,
her cape flying in the prairie wind.

The train slowly gathers momentum,
but birds blacken the window
and outpace the train.

The man is searching for the woman
in the frenzy of feathers.
The tracks narrow to a single destination.

PRETENDING

Pretending before believing,
that's how I became someone else.

I imagined I had changed. I imagined it
so hard and so long, so long and so hard.

I was the crepe myrtle willing
bare branches into crimson ruffles.

I was an actor playing a part.
Now I'm the author writing the lines.

I had trouble believing it
until you believed it.

You called me by another name,
and my head snapped round to answer.

You took off my mask
and kissed the mask underneath.

The steam cleared in the bathroom mirror
and a face appeared.

It was a face I had never seen.
It was mine, the face I'd always wanted.

PROGNOSTICATION

A magician jumped out of the hedge and blocked my way.
A half penny to tell your fortune, he cried,
his one good eye rolling in its socket,
and a thousand lira if I succeed.
It was worth half a penny just to hear him out.
He pulled a vial from his pocket and poured oil in the ditch.
He asked me to stare deep into that slimy mirror.
I was surprised to see myself in a fast-forward movie:
baby, child, student, newlywed, mother, retiree, corpse.
That will be a thousand lira, please, he said triumphantly.
That's not a prophecy, I objected; that could happen to anyone.
The magician just laughed.
You think you're so different from everyone else?

THE MONK AND THE RABBIT

This story was told to me by a wanderer, but I believe it to be true:
There once was a monk who lived in seclusion with his prayers.

The farmers in the valley thought the temple was a ruin,
what with the swallow nests where the walls had lost their stones.

Rarely was the monk seen in the forest and when seen he would hide.
Never was a light seen in his dwelling, and no sound was ever heard.

It was said he would at times appear in the night at a villager's window
leaving a drift of green light and blue dust behind the next morning

The rabbit had a hankering for the wild cabbage that grew only
among the parasol mushrooms in the forest's jellied shadows.

He crouched at the woods' edge, where rabbits seldom went.
His ears stiffened and his nose twitched, keen for signs of cabbage.

Every morning the monk would wake with a new prayer in his head.
He'd quickly ink it into his bedside notebook before slipping on his sandals.

One day upon rising he spied through the curtains and what did he see as
the sun pierced his window but a half rabbit-half man approaching.

It was the cabbage that turned the bunny into a human,
and it was this stranger who turned the monk's prayers into poems.

And it was poems that repaired the temple: thatch on the roof,
plaster on the ceiling, lanterns in the windows.

SAFETY

She wore a newspaper hat, hedgehog mittens
and a dress made entirely of safety pins,
which sparkled silver in the morning sun.

I couldn't help myself; I followed her
down a road without signs to a town without cafes
up five flights of stairs to her garret.

She served thistle tea with stinging nettles.
She claimed her dead dog and cat
were company enough.

But she sat next to me on her couch,
and with each sip of tea,
the pins shone brighter and sang louder.

When I took her in my arms and kissed her,
safety pins suddenly snapped open and stabbed me.
One hundred poppies bloomed on my white shirt and khakis.

Now open like little V's, the loosened pins
fell in a pile around her bare feet.
And so I removed my blood-stained clothes.

SAGUARO

The desert wren in the sandstone canyon
sings of the lost and those who will be lost—
she sings of those blinded by wind and by sand—
of the men who turned the river to blood—
of the saints and prophets
who wander parched through the dunes—
of the prospector in fluttering rags—
of those who fall to their knees
of those who sip from the poisoned river—
of those who know the secret springs.

The tiny bird in the saguaro cactus
hums the high note of lost mirages
and the low note of travelers far from home,
the rapid rhythm of wings in flight,
the slow hymn of the watchful perch.

This canyon is a cathedral without doors,
a temple without tablets,
a reservoir of light.
From its thorny pulpit, the wren cries,
I too have swallowed the sun.

ICARUS

The grove is full of cedar waxwings,
an orchard of lemons with brown wings,
hatchet hats and scat singing,
butter on their breasts,
butter in their songs,
butter on the fingers of the humans below.

He fumbles with the buttons on her blouse.
She fumbles with the buttons on his shirt.
They both fumble for the right words.
He says what he believes she should be thinking.
She thinks what she believes he should be saying.

They tumble onto the crumbling leaves
and fumble their way to glory.
The songbirds spread their waxen wings
and fly into the sinking sun.

SUBJUNCTIVE

If I told you the truth, I could cross the border without papers.
If you told me your secret, it would bend my back.
If we lose control of our past, the horizons will close in.
If I distract you from the bear, you will take the wrong trail.
If you draw my attention to the funnel cloud, I will jump down the well.
If we lose sight of the future, our compass will be useless.
If our lives have no heart, this poem will be hypothetical.
If this poem had no head, it would merely be confessional.
If the river had no mouth, words would flood the banks.
If the banks had no tellers, who could tell us what we're worth?

TAKE MY HAND

I hate it when you act as if there's no death,
leaving me alone in this house.

I hate this silence of muffled bells,
stoic uncles and veiled aunts.

Don't strap me in the parlor chair,
rocking back and forth, back and forth.

I can't say goodbye
till you say goodbye.

Stop watering the flowers.
Stop answering the phone.

There must be a black hat you can wear,
a black coat against the chill.

There must be a song you know,
slow and in a minor key.

I can't open the front door
till you close the lid.

If you throw a fistful of dirt,
I'll take your muddied hand.

We will walk down the to the dock
and gaze at the far islands.

THIS SOLID EARTH

I thought it was the safest place in all the world
until this morning when the earthquake struck.
I hadn't known the ocean could rise so high.
I hadn't imagined the land could sink so low.
No warning siren, no worried meetings,
everything can be taken away in a minute.
A ceiling beam lands on the marriage bed;
my childhood windows splinter on the floor.
My face, my hands, my hair caked with matted dust,
It has to be washed in the river.
It has to be removed from the bloodstream.
It has to be dreamed from the mind.
Our first-edition books swept out with the sheetrock.
I let go of all my listening, all my seeing.
The future requires a whole new calendar.
And so does the past.

A YEAR LATER

A lantern in a rainy night
is all I ask of you,
a cookie from the dozens,
a glove to tame the foal.

I have walked two hours
to reach this stand of oaks.
I shake out my umbrella and listen
for the sound of your green shoes.

In my black satchel are the silver spoons
I scooped from off your table.
I can return these and the candlesticks,
but not the name I dirtied with my hands.

Unwind your long woolen scarf.
Release the doves in your sleeves.
Come sit on this red bench with me.
There is nothing more to fear.

It's true I robbed you once of everything
but I'm a different man now.
There are violets in my buttonhole
and lemon drops in my palm.

THE STORY WITHOUT END

She found love's agony in January
when creek turned hard as stone.

She found love's ecstasy in February
when sky was washed deep clean.

She found love's birth in March
when bear peeked out of cave.

She found love's rapture in April
when maple unfolded green.

She found love's ache in May
when lilacs awaited bees.

She found love's joy in June
when peach juice ran in rivers.

She found love's melancholy in July
When slow koi hid in shadows.

She found love's delight in August
when sunflowers tangled foxtail.

She found love's torture in September
when bent reapers scythed cane.

She found love's wonder in October
when silver trunks sprung amber leaves.

She found love's hunger in November
when baby wolves crossed empty snowscape.

She found love's splendor in December
when ice twigs captured morning light.

Acknowledgments

Grateful acknowledgement to the publisher and editors of Italo Calvino's *Folktales*, from which we adapted prose into poetry as the source for our innovations: Calvino, Italo. *Italian Folktales*, Selected and Retold by Italo Calvino (translated by George Martin). Harcourt Brace Jovanovich, New York and London, 1980.

About the Authors

GRACE CAVALIERI was Maryland's tenth Poet Laureate (2018-2024.) Her new poetry book: *Owning The Not So Distant World* won the Blue Light Book Award, (2024) and *The Long Game: Poems Selected & New* was published in 2023. She founded and still produces *The Poet and the Poem* for public radio, now from the Library of Congress, celebrating 48 years on-air in 2025. Grace was formerly Asst Director for Children's Programming, Corporate PBS., and senior media officer, NEH. Among honors, She holds the Bordighera Award, two Allen Ginsberg Awards and the CPB Silver Medal. She's an Academy of American Poets Fellow.

GEOFFREY HIMES's poetry has been published by Best American Poetry, December, Redactions, Gianthology, the Loch Raven Review, Pendemics, Survision, Innisfree, Salt Lick, Cathexis Northwest, Gargoyle and other publications. His poems are included in several anthologies, including *Baltimorology, Singing in the Dark*, and *Speaking for Everyone*. His song lyrics have been set to music by Si Kahn, Walter Egan, Sonia, Billy Kemp, Fred Koller and others. He has written about popular music, film, theater and books for the Washington Post, New York Times, Rolling Stone, Smithsonian Magazine, Paste, Downbeat, Sing Out, No Depression and many others since 1977. His book on Bruce Springsteen, *Born in the USA*, was published in 2005. His book on Emmylou Harris and Rosanne Cash, *In-Law Country*, was published in 2024.

VIA Folios
A refereed book series dedicated to the culture of Italians and Italian Americans.

LAURETTE FOLK. *Eleison*. Vol. 177. Novel.
FRANCES NEVILL. *Coquina Soup*. Vol. 176. Literature.
FRANCINE MASIELLO. *The Tomb of the Divers*. Vol. 175. Novel.
PIETRO DI DONATO. *Collected Stories*. Vol. 174. Literature.
RACHEL GUIDO deVRIES. *The Birthday Years*. Vol. 173. Poetry.
MATTHEW MEDURI. *Collegiate Gothic*. Vol. 172. Novel.
THOMAS RUGGIO. *Finding Dandini*. Vol. 171. Art History.
TAMBURRI GIORDANO GARDAPHÈ. *From the Margin*. Vol. 170. Anthology.
ANNA MONARDO. *After Italy*. Vol. 169. Memoir.
JOEY NICOLETTI. *Extinction Wednesday*. Vol. 168. Poetry.
MARIA FAMÀ. *Trigger*. Vol. 167. Poetry.
WILLI Q MINN. *What? Nothing*. Vol. 166. Poetry.
RICHARD VETERE. *She's Not There*. Vol. 165. Literature.
FRANK GIOIA. *Mercury Man*. Vol. 164. Literature.
LUISA M. GIULIANETTI. *Agrodolce*. Vol. 163. Literature.
ANGELO ZEOLLA. *The Bronx Unbound ovvero i versi bronxesi*. Vol. 162. Poetry.
NICHOLAS A. DiCHARIO. *Giovanni's Tree*. Vol. 161. Literature.
ADELE ANNESI. *What She Takes Away*. Vol. 160. Novel.
ANNIE RACHELE LANZILLOTTO. *Whaddyacall the Wind?*. Vol. 159. Memoir.
JULIA LISELLA. *Our Lively Kingdom*. Vol. 158. Poetry.
MARK CIABATTARI. *When the Mask Slips*. Vol. 157. Novel.
JENNIFER MARTELLI. *The Queen of Queens*. Vol. 156. Poetry.
TONY TADDEI. *The Sons of the Santorelli*. Vol. 155. Literature.
FRANCO RICCI. *Preston Street • Corso Italias*. Vol. 154. History.
MIKE FIORITO. *The Hated Ones*. Vol. 153. Literature.
PATRICIA DUNN. *Last Stop on the 6*. Vol. 152. Novel.
WILLIAM BOELHOWER. *Immigrant Autobiography*. Vol. 151. Literary Criticism.
MARC DIPAOLO. *Fake Italian*. Vol. 150. Literature.
GAIL REITANO. *Italian Love Cake*. Vol. 149. Novel.
VINCENT PANELLA. *Sicilian Dreams*. Vol. 148. Novel.
MARK CIABATTARI. *The Literal Truth: Rizzoli Dreams of Eating the Apple of Earthly Delights*. Vol. 147. Novel.
MARK CIABATTARI. *Dreams of An Imaginary New Yorker Named Rizzoli*. Vol. 146. Novel.
LAURETTE FOLK. *The End of Aphrodite*. Vol. 145. Novel.
ANNA CITRINO. *A Space Between*. Vol. 144. Poetry
MARIA FAMÀ. *The Good for the Good*. Vol. 143. Poetry.
ROSEMARY CAPPELLO. *Wonderful Disaster*. Vol. 142. Poetry.
B. AMORE. *Journeys on the Wheel*. Vol. 141. Poetry.
ALDO PALAZZESCHI. *The Manifestos of Aldo Palazzeschi*. Vol 140. Literature.
ROSS TALARICO. *The Reckoning*. Vol 139. Poetry.
MICHELLE REALE. *Season of Subtraction*. Vol 138. Poetry.

MARISA FRASCA. *Wild Fennel.* Vol 137. Poetry.
RITA ESPOSITO WATSON. *Italian Kisses.* Vol. 136. Memoir.
SARA FRUNER. *Bitter Bites from Sugar Hills.* Vol. 135. Poetry.
KATHY CURTO. *Not for Nothing.* Vol. 134. Memoir.
JENNIFER MARTELLI. *My Tarantella.* Vol. 133. Poetry.
MARIA TERRONE. *At Home in the New World.* Vol. 132. Essays.
GIL FAGIANI. *Missing Madonnas.* Vol. 131. Poetry.
LEWIS TURCO. *The Sonnetarium.* Vol. 130. Poetry.
JOE AMATO. *Samuel Taylor's Hollywood Adventure.* Vol. 129. Novel.
BEA TUSIANI. *Con Amore.* Vol. 128. Memoir.
MARIA GIURA. *What My Father Taught Me.* Vol. 127. Poetry.
STANISLAO PUGLIESE. *A Century of Sinatra.* Vol. 126. Popular Culture.
TONY ARDIZZONE. *The Arab's Ox.* Vol. 125. Novel.
PHYLLIS CAPELLO. *Packs Small Plays Big.* Vol. 124. Literature.
FRED GARDAPHÉ. *Read 'em and Reap.* Vol. 123. Criticism.
JOSEPH A. AMATO. *Diagnostics.* Vol 122. Literature.
DENNIS BARONE. *Second Thoughts.* Vol 121. Poetry.
OLIVIA K. CERRONE. *The Hunger Saint.* Vol 120. Novella.
GARIBLADI M. LAPOLLA. *Miss Rollins in Love.* Vol 119. Novel.
JOSEPH TUSIANI. *A Clarion Call.* Vol 118. Poetry.
JOSEPH A. AMATO. *My Three Sicilies.* Vol 117. Poetry & Prose.
MARGHERITA COSTA. *Voice of a Virtuosa and Coutesan.* Vol 116. Poetry.
NICOLE SANTALUCIA. *Because I Did Not Die.* Vol 115. Poetry.
MARK CIABATTARI. *Preludes to History.* Vol 114. Poetry.
HELEN BAROLINI. *Visits.* Vol 113. Novel.
ERNESTO LIVORNI. *The Fathers' America.* Vol. 112. Poetry.
MARIO B. MIGNONE. *The Story of My People.* Vol 111. Non-fiction.
GEORGE GUIDA. *The Sleeping Gulf.* Vol 110. Poetry.
JOEY NICOLETTI. *Reverse Graffiti.* Vol 109. Poetry.
GIOSE RIMANELLI. *Il mestiere del furbo.* Vol 108. Criticism.
LEWIS TURCO. *The Hero Enkidu.* Vol 107. Poetry.
AL TACCONELLI. *Perhaps Fly.* Vol 106. Poetry.
RACHEL GUIDO DEVRIES. *A Woman Unknown in Her Bones.* Vol 105. Poetry.
BERNARD BRUNO. *A Tear and a Tear in My Heart.* Vol 104. Non-fiction.
FELIX STEFANILE. *Songs of the Sparrow.* Vol. 103. Poetry.
FRANK POLIZZI. *A New Life with Bianca.* Vol 102. Poetry.
GIL FAGIANI. *Stone Walls.* Vol 101. Poetry.
LOUISE DESALVO. *Casting Off.* Vol 100. Fiction.
MARY JO BONA. *I Stop Waiting for You.* Vol 99. Poetry.
RACHEL GUIDO DEVRIES. *Stati zitt, Josie.* Vol 98. Children's Literature. $8
GRACE CAVALIERI. *The Mandate of Heaven.* Vol 97. Poetry.
MARISA FRASCA. *Via incanto.* Vol 96. Poetry.
DOUGLAS GLADSTONE. *Carving a Niche for Himself.* Vol 95. History.
MARIA TERRONE. *Eye to Eye.* Vol 94. Poetry.
CONSTANCE SANCETTA. *Here in Cerchio.* Vol 93. Local History.
MARIA MAZZIOTTI GILLAN. *Ancestors' Song.* Vol 92. Poetry.

MICHAEL PARENTI. *Waiting for Yesterday: Pages from a Street Kid's Life.* Vol 90. Memoir.
ANNIE LANZILLOTTO. *Schistsong.* Vol 89. Poetry.
EMANUEL DI PASQUALE. *Love Lines.* Vol 88. Poetry.
CAROSONE & LOGIUDICE. *Our Naked Lives.* Vol 87. Essays.
JAMES PERICONI. *Strangers in a Strange Land: A Survey of Italian-Language American Books.* Vol 86. Book History.
DANIELA GIOSEFFI. *Escaping La Vita Della Cucina.* Vol 85. Essays.
MARIA FAMÀ. *Mystics in the Family.* Vol 84. Poetry.
ROSSANA DEL ZIO. *From Bread and Tomatoes to Zuppa di Pesce "Ciambotto".* Vol. 83. Memoir.
LORENZO DELBOCA. *Polentoni.* Vol 82. Italian Studies.
SAMUEL GHELLI. *A Reference Grammar.* Vol 81. Italian Language.
ROSS TALARICO. *Sled Run.* Vol 80. Fiction.
FRED MISURELLA. *Only Sons.* Vol 79. Fiction.
FRANK LENTRICCHIA. *The Portable Lentricchia.* Vol 78. Fiction.
RICHARD VETERE. *The Other Colors in a Snow Storm.* Vol 77. Poetry.
GARIBALDI LAPOLLA. *Fire in the Flesh.* Vol 76 Fiction & Criticism.
GEORGE GUIDA. *The Pope Stories.* Vol 75 Prose.
ROBERT VISCUSI. *Ellis Island.* Vol 74. Poetry.
ELENA GIANINI BELOTTI. *The Bitter Taste of Strangers Bread.* Vol 73. Fiction.
PINO APRILE. *Terroni.* Vol 72. Italian Studies.
EMANUEL DI PASQUALE. *Harvest.* Vol 71. Poetry.
ROBERT ZWEIG. *Return to Naples.* Vol 70. Memoir.
AIROS & CAPPELLI. *Guido.* Vol 69. Italian/American Studies.
FRED GARDAPHÉ. *Moustache Pete is Dead! Long Live Moustache Pete!.* Vol 67. Literature/Oral History.
PAOLO RUFFILLI. *Dark Room/Camera oscura.* Vol 66. Poetry.
HELEN BAROLINI. *Crossing the Alps.* Vol 65. Fiction.
COSMO FERRARA. *Profiles of Italian Americans.* Vol 64. Italian Americana.
GIL FAGIANI. *Chianti in Connecticut.* Vol 63. Poetry.
BASSETTI & D'ACQUINO. *Italic Lessons.* Vol 62. Italian/American Studies.
CAVALIERI & PASCARELLI, Eds. *The Poet's Cookbook.* Vol 61. Poetry/Recipes.
EMANUEL DI PASQUALE. *Siciliana.* Vol 60. Poetry.
NATALIA COSTA, Ed. *Bufalini.* Vol 59. Poetry.
RICHARD VETERE. *Baroque.* Vol 58. Fiction.
LEWIS TURCO. *La Famiglia/The Family.* Vol 57. Memoir.
NICK JAMES MILETI. *The Unscrupulous.* Vol 56. Humanities.
BASSETTI. ACCOLLA. D'AQUINO. *Italici: An Encounter with Piero Bassetti.* Vol 55. Italian Studies.
GIOSE RIMANELLI. *The Three-legged One.* Vol 54. Fiction.
CHARLES KLOPP. *Bele Antiche Stòrie.* Vol 53. Criticism.
JOSEPH RICAPITO. *Second Wave.* Vol 52. Poetry.
GARY MORMINO. *Italians in Florida.* Vol 51. History.
GIANFRANCO ANGELUCCI. *Federico F.* Vol 50. Fiction.
ANTHONY VALERIO. *The Little Sailor.* Vol 49. Memoir.

ROSS TALARICO. *The Reptilian Interludes.* Vol 48. Poetry.
RACHEL GUIDO DE VRIES. *Teeny Tiny Tino's Fishing Story.*
  Vol 47. Children's Literature.
EMANUEL DI PASQUALE. *Writing Anew.* Vol 46. Poetry.
MARIA FAMÀ. *Looking For Cover.* Vol 45. Poetry.
ANTHONY VALERIO. *Toni Cade Bambara's One Sicilian Night.* Vol 44. Poetry.
EMANUEL CARNEVALI. *Furnished Rooms.* Vol 43. Poetry.
BRENT ADKINS. et al., Ed. *Shifting Borders. Negotiating Places.*
  Vol 42. Conference.
GEORGE GUIDA. *Low Italian.* Vol 41. Poetry.
GARDAPHÈ, GIORDANO, TAMBURRI. *Introducing Italian Americana.*
  Vol 40. Italian/American Studies.
DANIELA GIOSEFFI. *Blood Autumn/Autunno di sangue.* Vol 39. Poetry.
FRED MISURELLA. *Lies to Live By.* Vol 38. Stories.
STEVEN BELLUSCIO. *Constructing a Bibliography.* Vol 37. Italian Americana.
ANTHONY JULIAN TAMBURRI, Ed. *Italian Cultural Studies 2002.*
  Vol 36. Essays.
BEA TUSIANI. *con amore.* Vol 35. Memoir.
FLAVIA BRIZIO-SKOV, Ed. *Reconstructing Societies in the Aftermath of War.*
  Vol 34. History.
TAMBURRI. et al., Eds. *Italian Cultural Studies 2001.* Vol 33. Essays.
ELIZABETH G. MESSINA, Ed. *In Our Own Voices.*
  Vol 32. Italian/American Studies.
STANISLAO G. PUGLIESE. *Desperate Inscriptions.* Vol 31. History.
HOSTERT & TAMBURRI, Eds. *Screening Ethnicity.*
  Vol 30. Italian/American Culture.
G. PARATI & B. LAWTON, Eds. *Italian Cultural Studies.* Vol 29. Essays.
HELEN BAROLINI. *More Italian Hours.* Vol 28. Fiction.
FRANCO NASI, Ed. *Intorno alla Via Emilia.* Vol 27. Culture.
ARTHUR L. CLEMENTS. *The Book of Madness & Love.* Vol 26. Poetry.
JOHN CASEY, et al. *Imagining Humanity.* Vol 25. Interdisciplinary Studies.
ROBERT LIMA. *Sardinia/Sardegna.* Vol 24. Poetry.
DANIELA GIOSEFFI. *Going On.* Vol 23. Poetry.
ROSS TALARICO. *The Journey Home.* Vol 22. Poetry.
EMANUEL DI PASQUALE. *The Silver Lake Love Poems.* Vol 21. Poetry.
JOSEPH TUSIANI. *Ethnicity.* Vol 20. Poetry.
JENNIFER LAGIER. *Second Class Citizen.* Vol 19. Poetry.
FELIX STEFANILE. *The Country of Absence.* Vol 18. Poetry.
PHILIP CANNISTRARO. *Blackshirts.* Vol 17. History.
LUIGI RUSTICHELLI, Ed. *Seminario sul racconto.* Vol 16. Narrative.
LEWIS TURCO. *Shaking the Family Tree.* Vol 15. Memoirs.
LUIGI RUSTICHELLI, Ed. *Seminario sulla drammaturgia.*
  Vol 14. Theater/Essays.
FRED GARDAPHÈ. *Moustache Pete is Dead! Long Live Moustache Pete!.*
  Vol 13. Oral Literature.
JONE GAILLARD CORSI. *Il libretto d'autore. 1860 - 1930.* Vol 12. Criticism.

HELEN BAROLINI. *Chiaroscuro: Essays of Identity.* Vol 11. Essays.
PICARAZZI & FEINSTEIN, Eds. *An African Harlequin in Milan.* Vol 10. Theater/Essays.
JOSEPH RICAPITO. *Florentine Streets & Other Poems.* Vol 9. Poetry.
FRED MISURELLA. *Short Time.* Vol 8. Novella.
NED CONDINI. *Quartettsatz.* Vol 7. Poetry.
ANTHONY JULIAN TAMBURRI, Ed. *Fuori: Essays by Italian/American Lesbiansand Gays.* Vol 6. Essays.
ANTONIO GRAMSCI. P. Verdicchio. Trans. & Intro. *The Southern Question.* Vol 5. Social Criticism.
DANIELA GIOSEFFI. *Word Wounds & Water Flowers.* Vol 4. Poetry. $8
WILEY FEINSTEIN. *Humility's Deceit: Calvino Reading Ariosto Reading Calvino.* Vol 3. Criticism.
PAOLO A. GIORDANO, Ed. *Joseph Tusiani: Poet. Translator. Humanist.* Vol 2. Criticism.
ROBERT VISCUSI. *Oration Upon the Most Recent Death of Christopher Columbus.* Vol 1. Poetry.

www.ingramcontent.com/pod-product-compliance
Lightning Source LLC
Chambersburg PA
CBHW022118090426
42743CB00008B/898